Heaven Milkshake in a Glass

Delicious Chocolate Milkshake Recipes
to Satisfy Your Cravings

Table of Contents

Introduction

Are you a chocolate lover looking for new and delicious ways to enjoy your favorite flavor?

Do you want to make amazing chocolate milkshakes right in your own kitchen?

Do you need some inspiration for your next chocolate dessert?

If you answered yes to any of these questions, then Heaven in Milkshake a Glass is for you!

Heaven Milkshake in a Glass is the perfect way to enjoy a delicious chocolatey treat. Inside, you'll find several recipes for delicious chocolate milkshakes, made with a variety of chocolate flavors. There are recipes for classic chocolate milkshakes, as well as more creative flavor combinations like peanut butter and chocolate, strawberry and Chocolate , and even Chocolate banana peanut butter milkshake. Each recipe includes easy-to-follow instructions, so you can make the perfect milkshake every time. Whether you're looking for a fun snack or a special treat, this cookbook has you covered.

Features:

- Delicious chocolate milkshake recipes
- A variety of amazing flavor combinations, so you can find the perfect one for you
- Beautiful photos of each recipe, so you can see exactly what your milkshake will look like
- Easy-to-follow instructions for perfect results every time
- Perfect for a weekend treat or a fun snack

We want you to have the best possible experience when using our cookbook, which is why each recipe has been tested and perfected before it was included.

So go ahead and add this beautiful book to your kitchen collection today!

Recipe 1. Chocolate Banana Peanut Butter Milkshake

Preparation Time-10 minutes

Servings-1

Ingredient List:

1. ½ ounce honey

2. 1 scoop chocolate-flavored protein powder

3. 1 ounce smooth peanut butter

4. 6 ice cubes

5.   8 ounces milk

6.   1 teaspoon unsweetened cocoa powder

7.   1 medium banana

Instructions:

Step 1   Mix all ingredients in a food processor or
           blender and process until smooth. Pour into
           milkshake glasses and serve.

Recipe 2. Ricotta Mochaccino Milkshake

Preparation Time-15 minutes

Servings-3

Ingredient List:

1. 4 ounces partly-skim ricotta cheese
2. 1 tray ice cubes
3. ½ ounce unsweetened cocoa powder
4. 1/4 teaspoon vanilla extract

5. 16 ounces strong chilled brewed coffee

6. ½ ounce powdered coffee creamer

7. 2 packets artificial sweetener

Instructions:

Step 1   Pour coffee into a blender or food processor and add the rest of the ingredients, finishing with the ice cubes. Process until smooth. Pour into tall glasses and serve.

Recipe 3. Chocolate Banana Latte Milkshake

Preparation Time-10 minutes

Servings-2

Ingredient List:

1. 4 ounces cold coffee

2. 1 ½ ounces vanilla ice cream

3. 1 ½ ounces chocolate syrup

4. 4 ounces milk

5. 1 large banana

6. 16 ounces crushed ice

Instructions:

Step 1   Mix milk, coffee, banana, vanilla ice cream, syrup, and crushed ice in a food processor or blender and process until smooth. Pour into milkshake glasses and serve.

Recipe 4. Chocolate Buzz Milkshake

Preparation Time-5 minutes

Servings-2

Ingredient List:

1. 8 ounces milk

2. 1 ounce espresso coffee

3. 5 ice cubes

4. 6 ounces chocolate ice cream

5. 1 ounce chocolate syrup

6.   1/3 ounce instant hot chocolate mix

Instructions:

Step 1   Mix milk, ice cubes, and coffee in a blender or food
          processor and process until smooth and creamy.
          Add ice cream, chocolate powder, and syrup and
          process again until combined and smooth.
Step 2   Pour into tall glasses and serve.

Recipe 5. Iced Mochas

Preparation Time-15 minutes

Servings-4

Ingredient List:

1. 2 ounces chocolate syrup

2. 16 ounces milk

3. 2 ounces white sugar

4. 12 ounces strong chilled brewed coffee

Instructions:

Step 1 Pour chilled coffee into an ice cube tray and freeze overnight.

Step 2 Combine frozen coffee cubes, syrup, milk, and white sugar in a food processor or blender and process until smooth. Pour into tall glasses and serve.

Recipe 6. Epic Strawberry Chocolate Milkshake

Preparation Time-5 minutes

Servings-2

Ingredient List:

1. 1 ripened banana

2. 24 ounces 3% milk

3. 8 ounces strawberry ice cream

4. 1 ounce chocolate dessert sauce

Instructions:

Step 1   Combine banana, 3% milk, strawberry ice cream, and dessert sauce in a blender and process until smooth. Then pour into tall glasses and serve.

Recipe 7. Frozen Hot Chocolate

Preparation Time-15 minutes

Servings-2

Ingredient List:

1. 1 ounce hot fudge topping
2. 12 ounces divided 2% milk
3. 24 ounces ice cubes
4. 1 ½ ounce milk chocolate candy bar
5. 1/3 ounce instant hot chocolate mix

Instructions:

Step 1   Place chocolate bar and fudge topping in a microwave-safe bowl. Cook in the microwave for 1-2 minutes on High in 20-second intervals. Stir well in between each interval and continue this process until melted completely and smooth. Don't overcook!

Step 2   Stir in 4 ounces of milk and hot chocolate mix into the hot melted chocolate mixture until fully combined. Cool for 10-15 minutes.

Step 3   Pour the mixture from the bowl into a blender or food processor with the rest of the ingredients and process until smooth and creamy.

Step 4   Pour into 2 tall glasses and enjoy!

Recipe 8. Freeze-easy Chocolate Shake

Preparation Time-5 minutes

Servings-1

Ingredient List:

1. 8 ounces milk

2. 16 ounces softened chocolate ice cream

3. ½ ounce chocolate syrup

Instructions:

Step 1   Mix ice cream with milk in a blender. Pour in the chocolate syrup and blend until smooth. Pour into a tall glass and enjoy.

Recipe 9. Vegan Avocado Chocolate Shake

Preparation Time-10 minutes

Servings-1

Ingredient List:

1. 8 ounces chocolate almond milk

2. 1/2 large, peeled banana, sliced and frozen solid

3. ½ ounce cocoa powder

4. 1 ripened peeled and pitted avocado, sliced and frozen solid

5. 1 ounce vegan hot fudge

Instructions:

Step 1   Place frozen avocado, frozen banana, cocoa powder, hot fudge sauce, and almond milk into a food processor or blender and process until smooth. Put all ingredients in a blender and combine until smooth. Pour into a tall glass and enjoy!

Recipe 10. Chocolate Peanut Butter Milkshake with Banana

Preparation Time-5 minutes

Servings-2

Ingredient List:

1. 2 ounces chocolate instant breakfast mix

2. 4 ice cubes

3. 2 sliced bananas

4. 1 ounce crunchy peanut butter

5. 16 ounces whole milk

Instructions:

Step 1   Mix all ingredients together in a food processor
and blender and process until smooth. Pour into
milkshake glasses and serve.

Recipe 11. Delicious Chocolate Milkshake

Preparation Time-5 minutes

Servings-1

Ingredient List:

1. 2 ounces milk

2. 8 ounces vanilla ice cream

3. 2 ounces semisweet chocolate chips

4. 1 ounce peanut butter

Instructions:

Step 1   Melt chocolate chips and peanut butter in the
microwave on high 1 minute in 20 second
increments until melted and creamy. Stir well in
between increments. Don't overcook!

Step 2   Mix vanilla ice cream, milk, and the melted
chocolate in a food processor or blender and
process until smooth and combined. Pour into a
tall glass and enjoy!

Recipe 12. Chocolate Strawberry Milkshake

Preparation Time-5 minutes

Servings-2

Ingredient List:

1. 4 ounces frozen strawberries
2. 1/3 ounce white sugar
3. 1/2 teaspoon vanilla extract
4. 8 ounces low-fat milk

5. ½ ripened banana

6. 1 ounce powdered chocolate drink mix

Method:

Step 1   Mix all ingredients in a food processor and blender and process until smooth. Add more strawberries if consistency is not thick enough. Pour glasses into milkshake glasses and serve.

Recipe 13. Thick Chocolate Milkshake

Preparation Time-5 minutes

Servings-2

Ingredient List:

1. 16 ounces vanilla ice cream

2. 2 ounces powdered chocolate drink mix

3. 4 ounces whole milk

4. 1 teaspoon powdered egg whites

Step 1   Mix all ingredients in a food processor or blender until smooth and thick. Stir in the ingredients to make sure it is evenly combined. Pour into milkshake glasses and serve.

Recipe 14. Delicious Chocolate Milkshake

Preparation Time-5 minutes

Servings-1

Ingredient List:

1. 1 ounce powdered chocolate drink mix
2. 2 scoops chocolate ice cream
3. 8 ounces whole milk

Instructions:

Step 1   Mix all ingredients in a food processor or blender and process until smooth. Pour into milkshake glasses and serve.

Recipe 15. Chocolate Mug Milkshake

Preparation Time-5 minutes

Servings-4

Ingredient List:

1. 32 ounces chocolate ice cream

2. 2 ounces brown sugar

3. 2 ounces white sugar

4. 16 ounces milk

5. 2 ounces ground cinnamon

Instructions:

Step 1   Mix all ingredients in a food processor or
         blender and process until smooth. Pour into
         milkshake glasses and serve.

Recipe 16. Iced Mocha Fusion Milkshake

Preparation Time-15 minutes

Servings-1

Ingredient List:

1. 1 teaspoon vanilla extract

2. 6 ounces milk

3. 1 ½ ounces granulated sugar

4. 8 ounces crushed ice

5. 1 ½ ounces instant coffee mix, mocha-flavored

Instructions:

Step 1   Combine all ingredients in a food processor or
blender and process until smooth. Pour mixture
into tall glasses and enjoy!

Recipe 17. Easy Chocolate Peanut Butter Milkshake

Preparation Time-15 minutes

Servings-2

Ingredient List:

1. 6 ounces unsweetened coconut milk

2. Chocolate sauce

3. Melted peanut butter

4. Chopped roasted peanuts

5. 8 ounces frozen chocolate peanut butter swirl coconut Milk

6. ½ ounce divided Cocowhip

Instructions:

Step 1   Combine frozen coconut milk and unsweetened coconut milk in a blender and process until smooth. Pour into tall glasses and top with CocoWhip. Drizzle with melted peanut butter, chocolate sauce, and chopped nuts.

Recipe 18. Zucchini Chocolate Banana Nut Milkshake

Preparation Time-5 minutes

Servings-4

Ingredient List:

1. 8 ounces grated frozen zucchini
2. 2 ounces chopped peanuts
3. 8 ounces half and half
4. 2 large, frozen ripened peeled bananas

5. 4 ounces sugar

6. 1 ounce cocoa powder

Instructions:

Step 1   Mix all ingredients in a blender or food
         processor and process until smooth. Pour into
         milkshake glasses and serve.

Recipe 19. Double Chocolate Milkshake

Preparation Time-10 minutes

Servings-2

Ingredient List:

1. 4 ounces whipped cream

2. ½ ounce chocolate shavings

3. 16 ounces premium quality chocolate ice cream

4. 2 diced dark chocolate candy bars, 1.65 ounces each

5. 2 ounces whipped cream

Instructions:

Step 1   Mix all ingredients except for chocolate
            shavings and whipped cream in a blender and
            process until fully incorporated and smooth.
            Pour into a tall glass and garnish with whipped
            cream and chocolate shavings.

Recipe 20. Chocolate Avocado Recipe

Preparation Time-10 minutes

Servings-2

Ingredient List:

1. 1 ripe peeled and pitted avocado, cut in half
2. 1 ounce melted non-dairy semisweet chocolate chips
3. 1 ½ ounces brown sugar
4. 12 ice cubes

5. 1 ½ ounces unsweetened cocoa powder

6. ½ ounce vanilla extract

7. 12 ounces vanilla almond milk

Instructions:

Step 1   Melt chocolate chips in the microwave on high in 20-second intervals until fully melted. Stir after every interval so as not to over-cook.

Step 2   Chop the avocado and place in a food processor or blender along with the melted chocolate and the rest of the Ingredients except for the ice. Process the mixture until smooth, add ice and pulse until the consistency is frosty and thick.

Recipe 21. Cold Cocoa Smoothie

Preparation Time-5 minutes

Servings-1

Ingredient List:

1. 2 ounces whipped cream
2. 1 ounce instant hot chocolate mix
3. 12 ounces vanilla ice cream
4. 12 ounces milk
5. 5 crushed Oreo cookies

Instructions:

Step 1   Combine vanilla ice cream, whipped cream, milk, chocolate mix, and Oreo cookies in a food processor or blender and process until smooth. Pour into a tall glass and enjoy!

Recipe 22. Chocolate Cheesecake Milkshake

Preparation Time-10 minutes

Servings-4

Ingredient List:

1. 16 ounces milk

2. 4 ounces softened cream cheese

3. 6 scoops chocolate ice cream

Instructions:

Step 1   Combine softened cream cheese and 8 ounces
of milk in a blender and process until smooth.
Add the rest of the ingredients and blend again
until combined and smooth. Pour into a tall
glass and serve.

Recipe 23. Chocolate Peppermint Milkshake

Preparation Time-10 minutes

Servings-1

Ingredient List:

1. 4 scoops softened vanilla bean ice cream

2. 3-4 drops red food coloring

3. 4 ounces skim milk

4. 1/2 teaspoon peppermint extract

5. ½ ounce high quality dark chocolate chips

6. 5 hard peppermint candies

7. 5-6 ice cubes

Instructions:

Step 1   Combine ice, candies, and chocolate chips in a food processor or blender and process until incorporated and little grainy. Add the rest of the ingredients except for milk and blend until smooth. Add milk and blend again until smooth and creamy.

Step 2   Pour into a tall glass and enjoy.

Recipe 24. Lighter Chocolate Milkshake

Preparation Time-10 minutes

Servings-2

Ingredient List:

1. 8 ounces coconut milk

2. 16 ounces ice cubes

3. 1 ounce unsweetened cocoa powder

4. ½ ounce smooth peanut butter

5. 1 chunked ripened banana

6. 1 teaspoon agave syrup

Instructions:

Step 1   Combine milk, ripened banana, unsweetened
cocoa powder, peanut butter, syrup, and ice in a
food processor or blender and process until
smooth. Pour into tall glasses and serve.

Recipe 25. Chocolate Mint Milkshakes

Preparation Time-5 minutes

Servings-2

Ingredient List:

1. 2 ounces milk

2. 4 scoops vanilla ice cream

3. 1 drop peppermint extract

4. 2 ounces chocolate syrup

Instructions:

Step 1   Mix all ingredients in a food processor or blender and process until smooth. Transfer to milkshake glasses and serve with straws.

Recipe 26. Chocolate Surprise Milkshake

Preparation Time-5 minutes

Servings-2

Ingredient List:

1.   2 ½ ounces powdered chocolate drink mix

2.   2 ounces chocolate chips

3.   1/3 ounce milk

4.   5 ice cubes

5. 1 ounce chocolate syrup

6. 3 scoops chocolate ice cream

Instructions:

Step 1   Mix all ingredients together in a blender or food processor and process until smooth and creamy. Pour into milkshake glasses and serve.

Recipe 27. Chocolate Spinach Milkshake

Preparation Time-5 minutes

Servings-2

Ingredient List:

1. ¾ ounce smooth peanut butter
2. 24 ounces packed fresh spinach
3. ½ teaspoon ground cinnamon
4. ½ ripened banana

5. 8 ounces chocolate soy milk

Instructions:

Step 1   Combine all ingredients in a food processor or
          blender and process until smooth and creamy.
          Pour into tall glasses and serve.

Recipe 28. Cocoa Coffee Milkshake

Preparation Time-5 minutes

Servings-1

Ingredient List:

1. ½ ounce instant hot chocolate mix

2. 1 teaspoon vanilla extract

3. 8 ounces 2% milk

4. ½ ounce instant coffee granules

5. 16 ounces vanilla ice cream

Instructions:

Step 1   Combine all ingredients in a food processor and process until smooth. Pour into a tall glass and enjoy!

Recipe 29. Chocolate Peanut Butter Milkshake

Preparation Time-5 minutes

Servings-4

Ingredient List:

1. 2 ounces milk

2. 2 ounces chocolate syrup

3. 8 ounces creamy peanut butter

4. 1 dozen ice cubes

Instructions:

Step 1   Mix all ingredients in a food processor or
blender and process until smooth.

Recipe 30. 3-ingredient Frozen Hot Chocolate

Preparation Time-5 minutes

Servings-6

Ingredient List:

1. 24 ounces milk
2. 24 ounces ice cubes
3. 24 ounces hot cocoa mix

Instructions:

Step 1   Combine all ingredients in a food processor or
blender and process until fully incorporated,
smooth and creamy. Pour into tall glasses and
serve.